Science Questions

How Does a Tornado Form?

by Megan Cooley Peterson

Bullfrog Books

Ideas for Parents and Teachers

Bullfrog Books let children practice reading informational text at the earliest reading levels. Repetition, familiar words, and photo labels support early readers.

Before Reading

- Discuss the cover photo. What does it tell them?

- Look at the picture glossary together. Read and discuss the words.

Read the Book

- "Walk" through the book and look at the photos. Let the child ask questions. Point out the photo labels.

- Read the book to the child, or have him or her read independently.

After Reading

- Prompt the child to think more. Ask: Did you know about tornadoes before reading this book? What other kinds of storms would you like to learn about?

Bullfrog Books are published by Jump!
5357 Penn Avenue South
Minneapolis, MN 55419
www.jumplibrary.com

Library of Congress Cataloging-in-Publication Data

Names: Peterson, Megan Cooley, author.
Title: How does a tornado form? / by Megan Cooley Peterson.
Description: Minneapolis, MN: Jump!, Inc., [2024]
Series: Science questions | Includes index.
Audience: Ages 5–8
Identifiers: LCCN 2022047961 (print)
LCCN 2022047962 (ebook)
ISBN 9798885244848 (hardcover)
ISBN 9798885244855 (paperback)
ISBN 9798885244862 (ebook)
Subjects: LCSH: Tornadoes—Juvenile literature.
Classification: LCC QC955.2 .P486 2024 (print)
LCC QC955.2 (ebook)
DDC 551.55/3—dc23/eng20230111
LC record available at https://lccn.loc.gov/2022047961
LC ebook record available at https://lccn.loc.gov/2022047962

Editor: Jenna Gleisner
Designer: Emma Almgren-Bersie

Photo Credits: Justin Hobson/Shutterstock, cover; mdesigner125/iStock, 1, 15; OooddySmile Studio/Shutterstock, 3; Boris Mrdja/Shutterstock, 4; New Africa/Shutterstock, 5; Meindert van der Haven/iStock, 6–7, 23tr, 23bl; John Sirlin/Dreamstime, 8–9, 12–13, 23br; Jon Bilous/Shutterstock, 10–11, 23tl; joebelanger/iStock, 14; clintspencer/iStock, 16–17, 19; Martin Haas/Shutterstock, 18; Jason Whitman/iStock, 20–21; Minerva Studio/Shutterstock, 24.

Printed in the United States of America at Corporate Graphics in North Mankato, Minnesota.

Table of Contents

Spinning Air

Clouds fill the sky.

It gets dark.

Wind blows.

Rain falls.

Boom!

We hear thunder.

Lightning flashes.

It is a thunderstorm.

lightning

warm air ····▶

cold air ····▶

Warm air rises.

Cold air sinks.

Wind blows across.

The air spins.

It forms a tube.

The tube fills with waterdrops.

Is it a tornado?

Not yet!

It is a funnel cloud.

funnel
cloud

tornado

The funnel grows longer.
It touches the ground.
Now it is a tornado.

Some are wide.

14

Others are thin.

The wind pulls up dust.

dust

It picks up a car!

It blows over trees.
Buildings fall.

The storm loses warm air.

The clouds break up.

The tornado stops.

We clean up.

How a Tornado Forms

How does a tornado form? Take a look!

1. Warm air rises into a thunderstorm. Cold air sinks.

warm air

2. Strong winds blow across. The storm starts spinning.

cold air

3. Spinning air forms a funnel cloud. It fills with waterdrops.

4. The funnel cloud touches the ground. It is a tornado.

Picture Glossary

funnel cloud
A cloud shaped like a cone with an open top and bottom.

lightning
Flashes of light when electricity moves between clouds and the ground.

thunderstorm
A storm with heavy rain, thunder, and lightning.

tornado
A violent windstorm that appears as a dark funnel cloud and causes damage.

Index

To Learn More

FACT SURFER

Finding more information is as easy as 1, 2, 3.

❶ Go to www.factsurfer.com

❷ Enter "howdoesatornadoform" into the search box.

❸ Choose your book to see a list of websites.